HERO DOGS
Courageous Canines in Action

by Donna M. Jackson

 Megan Tingley Books

LITTLE, BROWN AND COMPANY

New York ✦ An AOL Time Warner Company

This book is dedicated to the memory of
Heather Smith, my cousin Michael Jammen's fiancée,
who died when terrorists hijacked
American Airlines Flight 11 from Boston
and crashed it into One World Trade Center.
The two had planned to marry in October 2002.

It's also dedicated to those who died so senselessly
that day and to the brave men, women, and canines
who worked so valiantly to save them.

— D. M. J.

A portion of the proceeds from this book will be donated to the Suffolk County SPCA, the organization that coordinated all of the medical care of search, rescue and recovery dogs at the World Trade Center after the Sept. 11, 2001, terrorist attacks.

A special thanks to Little, Brown's amazing Tingley team, especially Megan Tingley and Mary Gruetzke for their superb editorial guidance and constant support, and to Charlie and Chris Jackson, the top dogs in my life.

ACKNOWLEDGMENTS Many thanks to all those who offered their time and talent in creating this book, especially: Roy and Lois Gross, Dr. John Charos, Frank Shane, Bob Sessions, Gerry Fornino, David Lim, Carol-Ann De Maio Goheen, Stefanie Goheen, Carol Ann Arnim, Peter Rapalus, Paul O'Brien, Troy and Pam Sica and their son, Troy Joseph, Ted and Kay Stern, Jeff Eckland, Dave Paradysz, Keoki Flagg, Cindy Ehlers, Nancy Zuckerman, Josiah Whitaker, Chris Christensen, Debra Barnes, Michael Hingson, Joanne Ritter, Sara Cedar Miller, Ed Apple, Lisa Beckett, Megan Thomas, Debra Tosch, Dr. Barbara Kalvig, Luther Hansen and the U.S. Army Quartermaster Museum, Lynnette Spanola, Mary Flood, Chris Hanley, Wendy Shattil and Bob Rozinski, Cathy Travis, Camille Ruggiero at AP Wide World Photos, and FEMA's National Urban Search and Rescue teams and photographers.

First Edition.

Library of Congress Cataloging-in-Publication Data

Jackson, Donna M.
Hero dogs : courageous canines in action / Donna M. Jackson. — 1st ed.
p. cm.
Summary: Presents a variety of stories about working and rescue dogs who help humans in many ways,
such as those involved in the work at the World Trade Center site after the disaster of September 11, 2001.
ISBN 0-316-82681-2
1. Working dogs — Juvenile literature. 2. Animal heroes — Juvenile literature.
[1. Working dogs. 2. Rescue dogs. 3. Animal heroes.] I. Title.
SF428.2 .K36 2003
636.7 — dc21   2002028299
10 9 8 7 6 5 4 3 2 1
PHX
Printed in the United States of America

Designed by Amelia Lau Carling.
The text was set in Gill Sans Book, and the display type is Rockwell Extra Bold.

CONTENTS

Rescue workers at rest.

MAN'S BEST FRIEND

Dogs and humans. We're faithful companions, whether nuzzling up to each other on the sofa or working as partners on the job. The ancient Egyptians held dogs in such high esteem that they mummified and buried them with their owners, and the Romans immortalized hunting dogs in works of art. No one knows exactly how or why we first befriended one another, but ours is a long, loyal history.

During World War II, canines served in combat by working as scouts, messengers, and mine detectors. Here, a husky is groomed for inspection.

Balto's bravery earned him a permanent spot in New York City's Central Park.

*I*n 1925, a sled dog named Balto led his team through a blinding blizzard and minus-fifty-degree temperatures to deliver medicine to children sick with diphtheria in Nome, Alaska. The serum saved the children's lives and prevented the highly contagious disease from spreading. The event also led to the creation of Alaska's Iditarod sled dog race.

*D*uring World War II, the U.S. Army credited a dog named Chips with having saved lives by attacking an enemy machine-gun crew in Sicily and bringing about their surrender. To honor his work, Chips received the Silver Star and Purple Heart medals. Soon after, the military revoked the medals, saying they were for people, not dogs. However, Chips's comrades honored him in their own way, and in 1993, Disney made a movie called Chips the War Dog.

Canines served in World War II combat by working as scouts, messengers, and mine detectors. Here, an officer inspects some of the men and dogs of the 42nd Quartermaster/War Dog Platoon in Belgium.

Scientists prepared Laika for her mission in space. Her breed — also named Laika — is known for its endurance.

*O*n November 3, 1957, Laika became the first dog in space when the former Soviet Union launched her into orbit on Sputnik II. Although she died several days later while on the mission, Laika proved that animals — and most likely people — could live in space.

Research indicates that dogs evolved from wolves. Both are members of the Canidae family and like to travel in packs. "Canidae" is derived from the Latin word caninus, which means "dog."

Dogs evolved from wolves and most likely began roaming the earth in some form about 100,000 years ago, says geneticist Robert Wayne in the January 2002 issue of *National Geographic*. Many scientists think that's when wolves may have ventured into camps scavenging for food, and our ancestors welcomed them — especially the young and least threatening wolves. The relationship would have been mutually beneficial: while humans shared their leftovers, wolves — with their keen senses — provided humans with protection from other wild animals. It's believed that over the next thousands of years, humans tamed wolves by breeding for people-friendly traits, and their descendants developed into smaller, more dependent breeds.

CANINES WITH A CAUSE

Today, dogs enhance our lives in many ways, most commonly by becoming extended members of our families and showering us with unconditional love. A wet kiss on the cheek and a wag of the tail can brighten our days and, according to hospital and university studies, improve our overall health by relieving stress and lowering blood pressure.

Some dogs train to be companions to people with disabilities. Jack Warnock credits his canine companion, Ellie, with giving him renewed independence. "She makes me feel like I felt . . . when I wasn't disabled," he says.

Some dogs, however, separate themselves from the pack with their unique skills, special talents, and superior work ethic. They earn their treats as entertainers, like Lassie and Rin Tin Tin; as herd and livestock guardians; and as assistance dogs who see for the blind (guide dogs), hear for the deaf (hearing dogs), and reach out for the disabled (service dogs). Therapy dogs bring comfort to the sick, grieving, and lonely, while police dogs track suspected criminals and sniff out drugs, bombs, and crime-scene evidence. Still other canines work in the military detecting mines, guarding troops, and delivering important messages. A small percentage even sniff out termites for homeowners and detect underground gas pipeline leaks for companies.

Pair a person with a canine and you have a powerful partnership. As we discovered in ancient times, dogs depend on us for their survival, but we often depend on them for ours.

Partners in Crisis:
THE DOGS of SEPTEMBER 11, 2001

On September 11, 2001, when terrorists attacked the World Trade Center in New York and the Pentagon outside of Washington, D.C., officials called for dogs trained in search and rescue disaster work to comb through the wreckage for survivors. Given the amount of destruction at the site, these courageous canines and their handlers were our best hope of finding people alive.

"Dogs can cover large scales of area and detect someone thirty feet down," explains veterinarian John Charos of New York. "No human alone could cover that amount of space in such a short time."

A Colorado Task Force member crosses the rubble with her search dog.

Michael Hingson and Roselle escaped from the 78th floor of Tower One on September 11, 2001.

A GUIDING LIGHT

When puppy trainers Ted and Kay Stern of California watched the World Trade Center under attack on September 11, they immediately thought of their friend Michael Hingson and his guide dog, Roselle. The couple knew that Hingson, a sales manager who has been blind since birth, worked on the 78th floor of One World Trade Center. They also knew that three-year-old Roselle — the first guide dog they had trained as a puppy — would be by his side.

"We worried about them," Mrs. Stern says, "so we emailed Michael to make sure he and Roselle were all right." Hingson didn't reply that day, most likely because he, Roselle, and a colleague had already made their way out of the office after the initial explosion rocked the tower fifteen floors above them.

"I heard a loud noise like a bump and then a lot of shaking. It was worse than any earthquake I've ever experienced," Hingson explained to Guide Dogs for the Blind, the organization that had brought him and Roselle together nine months earlier. "The building started swaying, and the air was filled with smoke, fire, paper, and the smell of kerosene." After calling his wife, Karen, to let her know he was okay, Hingson grabbed Roselle's harness and the two headed for the stairway with coworker David Frank.

"[Roselle] knew something was different," Hingson recalled. "But she never freaked out and never lost her focus . . . I held on to Roselle with my left hand and the rail with my right, like I usually do when going down stairs."

By the time the pair reached the bottom of the building, they were having difficulty breathing, Hingson says. "We were both very hot and tired. Roselle was panting and wanted to drink the water that was pooled on the floor." About two blocks away from the site, Tower Two began to collapse. "We started running for the subway," Hingson says. Soon after, Tower One fell and blanketed them with ash. Through it all Roselle remained focused on her work, eventually guiding Hingson to safety.

TOP TRAINING

One reason why Roselle remained so calm amid the confusion was her early training with the Sterns, who began socializing and providing daily

Like all puppies, Roselle loved her chew toys.

obedience lessons for the yellow Lab when she was only eight weeks old. Labrador retrievers, golden retrievers, German shepherds, and Lab-golden mixes are among the best breeds for guide dog work because of their intelligence and stable personalities.

"Roselle was a very playful puppy," Mrs. Stern says. "She used to steal my slippers from the closet and run all around the house and try to play keep-away. Sometimes she tested the limits and tried to pretend that she didn't remember her lessons."

But Mrs. Stern knew better. Roselle was a smart pup, who ultimately

Hero in the making: Roselle traveled everywhere with the Sterns, including this Santa Barbara Bird Refuge.

learned her commands very well — all twenty-five of them. She would sit, stay, lay, and come when called without being distracted. Dropping pots and pans on the floor didn't even faze her.

Staying on task and ignoring distractions such as loud noises, unusual smells, and offers of food is an important skill for guide dogs, because their blind partners will follow their movements very closely. "You don't want a guide dog that likes to chase balls," Mrs. Stern says.

Another part of Roselle's training involved socialization, which meant she traveled just about everywhere with the Sterns. "Lots of people around town know Roselle," Mrs. Stern says. "We took her to grocery stores, movies, plays, concerts, restaurants, parades, and the beach." They even took her on an airplane to New York, where she lay at their feet in the main cabin. The more confusing and noisy the place, the better. "We wanted her to be at ease in any situation."

While living with the Sterns, Roselle learned to trust, love, and attach herself to humans. "We work to get the 'dog' out of the dog," Mrs. Stern says. "It's really important that they bond with humans and have a desire to please." The Sterns reinforced that desire by lavishing Roselle with verbal and physical praise for such good behaviors as staying off furniture, not begging for food, and "going to the bathroom" on command — things that can be awfully difficult for a puppy to do! After staying with the Sterns for about a year, Roselle returned to the Guide Dogs organization for about six months of advanced instruction. There, she learned how to work with a harness and respond to guide-work-specific commands, such as "forward," "right," "left," and "halt." As the training progressed, instructors introduced Roselle to more challenging experiences: boarding buses and subways, entering and exiting elevators, and walking in crowded malls.

"A guide dog is trained to lead a person from point A to point B in a straight line; to stop for all changes in elevation (curbs, stairs); and to lead their partner around obstacles, including overhead obstacles such as tree limbs," says Debra Barnes of Guide Dogs for the Blind.

Guide dogs also learn how to safely direct their handlers across busy intersections. At street crossings, their blind partners listen to the flow of traffic, decide when to proceed, and command the dog to move forward. If a dog sees a car approaching, however, it's trained to "intelligently disobey" its handler.

GRADUATION DAY

"We cried a lot when it was time to turn in Roselle for her advanced training," Mrs. Stern says. "However, when she graduated, we had the privilege of presenting her to Michael. That's when we cried tears of joy to see that little puppy emerge as a confident, capable service dog."

That's also when the Sterns made a new friend.

"Michael is a very inspiring man," Mrs. Stern says. "I'm not only happy that he and Roselle are partners, I'm grateful to know him." In fact, the Sterns visited Michael and Roselle in New York a few months before the World Trade Center tragedy.

"You can imagine how proud we are of that sweet puppy," says Mrs. Stern, "doing exactly what she was trained to do. We are proud of her and equally proud of Michael, because they were a team who worked together perfectly to do the right thing in an emergency. Neither partner could have done it alone."

Roselle was a "model" puppy!

Another guide dog led his blind partner to safety on September 11. When a plane hijacked by terrorists crashed into One World Trade Center, Omar Rivera, a systems designer from the Port Authority of New York and New Jersey, called on his dog, Salty, to guide him down seventy flights of stairs. "He was very nervous," Rivera told the New York Times, *"but he didn't run away." In fact, Salty refused to leave Rivera's side, even when someone tried to take his leash. Soon after the two escaped the building, it collapsed to the ground.*

HEROES AT GROUND ZERO AND THE PENTAGON

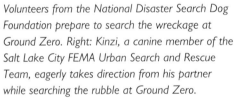

Volunteers from the National Disaster Search Dog Foundation prepare to search the wreckage at Ground Zero. Right: Kinzi, a canine member of the Salt Lake City FEMA Urban Search and Rescue Team, eagerly takes direction from his partner while searching the rubble at Ground Zero.

Chris Christensen felt his "heart pounding out of [his] chest" as he gazed at the ruins of the World Trade Center on September 13. "It looked like a bomb had gone off," he says. "You could smell the acrid smoke, and it literally burned your eyes as you walked up to the site."

Just two days earlier the police officer had watched his television in disbelief as the twin towers collapsed. That's when he decided to drive from his home in East Carondelet, Missouri, to New York City so he could assist in the rescue efforts. As always, his faithful partner, Servus — a nine-year-old Belgian Malinois (a Belgian shepherd) — accompanied him.

Servus, a specially trained search and rescue dog, was one of about 350 canine heroes from the United States and around the world who combed the ruins of the World Trade Center, searching for signs of survivors.

"Without the search and rescue dogs, there's no way we could have found anyone in the rubble," says Dr. John Charos, one of the lead veterinarians who coordinated the medical care for the dogs at Ground Zero. Even high-tech sensors can't replicate the sensory-detection abilities of a dog's nose, which is designed to receive and trap odors. While humans have an estimated 5 million scent receptors (cells used to smell), dogs have anywhere from 125 to 220 million, allowing them to pick up a scent up to half a mile away.

SUPER SNIFFERS

Most of the dogs who worked at the World Trade Center in the first few weeks were air-scenting dogs — dogs who use their noses to find people by picking up traces of human scent in the air, locating where it's most concentrated (called the scent cone), and following the scent to its source.

"When air-scenting dogs zero in on a human scent, they're really detecting dead skin cells," explains Bob Sessions, a veteran canine handler with the Maryland Task Force One FEMA Urban Search and Rescue Team. "The average human body sheds about 40,000 dead skin cells a minute. . . . These skin cells are covered

Rescue workers and a search dog emerge from the pile of rubble at the World Trade Center.

with bacteria, even on a person stepping out of the shower. The bacteria eat and digest the skin cells, giving off a gas that we call body odor." This body odor, mixed with other human scents, acts like an unseen cloud of smoke and is what the air-scenting dog targets, Sessions says.

Once a dog locates the scent of a trapped person, it signals its handler by barking. A second dog is then sent out to confirm the finding. In a disaster

Debra Tosch of the National Disaster Search Dog Foundation (NDSDF) and her dog, Abby, walk off "the pile" at Ground Zero. Abby's training on obstacle courses and rubble piles prepared her for work at the World Trade Center site.

Dogs certified by FEMA train regularly so that they'll be prepared to work during a disaster. Here, Thunder climbs a ladder and navigates the trees during a training session.

such as the World Trade Center, pinpointing the exact location of the scent is especially important, explains Sessions, because extricating a person from the debris can take hours and be highly dangerous.

"You don't just 'pull' people from the rubble," he says, "you have to remove the building from the person. It's like playing a game of pick-up sticks — it's extremely difficult and challenging, and you can't remove the wrong stick." If you remove the wrong piece of debris, the area could collapse, and people could get hurt.

READY TO SERVE

Along with having superior noses, search and rescue dogs working on disaster sites must be quick and nimble on their paws to safely navigate collapsed buildings and other dangerous situations. Dogs certified through the Federal Emergency Management Agency (FEMA) train regularly with their handlers so that when disaster strikes, they're fearless in the face of danger. Dark tunnels, extraordinary heights, wobbly surfaces, broken glass, and twisted metal do not daunt FEMA-certified dogs.

"There's no way you can prepare for something of this magnitude," says Debra Tosch of California, who worked at the World Trade Center with Abby, her four-year-old, FEMA-certified Labrador retriever. "However, because Abby had trained on obstacle courses and in rubble piles of buildings that were collapsed or torn down, she saw the site as a new 'playground' and had no trouble navigating it."

Abby's ladder-climbing skills also came in handy. In fact, one of the tests for FEMA certification involves walking up a ladder, crossing a plank that's six to eight feet off the ground, and then going down a ladder on the other side. "At the World Trade Center," says Tosch, "Abby crossed six-inch beams with thirty-foot drops and saw no difference — she just transferred her training."

FEMA-certified dogs such as Abby readily obey the voice commands of their handlers, such as "heel," "here," "down," and "stay," and they work well off-leash. "For instance," says Tosch, "Abby went across some of the beams a lot faster than I did, so I'd say 'wait,' and she'd sit and wait for me to cross. Then we'd move on."

Abby can follow hand signals, too. In the rubble, she moves left, right, backward, and forward according to Tosch's directions, and she stops what she's doing when she hears a whistle cue. Her excellent obedience and agility help to keep her safe.

"It's a team effort," says Tosch, who belongs to the National Disaster Search Dog Foundation (NDSDF) — an organization founded by Wilma Melville in 1995 to increase the number of certified disaster search dogs and trained handlers in the United States. "Over time, you really start to work well with each other and can read each other's body language," says Tosch. "I know when Abby's getting tired before she knows it."

Trust is part of the teamwork. "If Abby tells me nothing's there, then nothing's there. And if I send her into an area to search, she trusts that there's a good reason. The dogs use their noses, but we have to use our brains. It's a very strong combination if everything works right."

A rescue dog takes a well-deserved break from the search operations.

15

CALL TO THE PENTAGON

While Abby and other dogs searched for survivors at the World Trade Center, Gus and his handler, Ed Apple, worked at the Pentagon — the military headquarters of the United States. Located outside of Washington, D.C., the Pentagon also had been attacked by terrorists who hijacked a jetliner on September 11 and crashed it into part of the twenty-nine-acre complex. The next day, Apple and Gus arrived at the site with the Tennessee Task Force One FEMA Urban Search and Rescue Team. The two worked long days amid the smoke and lingering fumes of jet fuel, searching the hot zones — dangerous areas within the rubble. For this mission, Apple called on Gus to locate people who had lost their lives in the attack, because all hope of finding survivors had faded. Using voice and hand signals, he directed his FEMA-certified Lab through the "metal junkyard" of debris. When Gus barked to indicate a find, Apple would flag the spot so that detectives knew where to look. Workers also sent Gus to search hard-to-reach areas whenever they saw pieces of clothing or other indications of human life.

"Gus is a multitalented dog," says Apple. "At home, he works for the local sheriff department's emergency services team." There, he helps find missing persons, solve crimes, and recover drowning victims.

Above: Gus and his handler, Ed Apple of the Tennessee Task Force One FEMA Urban Search and Rescue Team, wait to enter the crash site at the Pentagon. Below: Gus and Apple search for victims amid the wreckage at the Pentagon. When Gus makes a find, he barks to alert Ed.

A night photo of the Pentagon shows the damage done when a commercial airliner hijacked by terrorists struck the building on September 11, 2001.

PUPPIES WITH POTENTIAL

Finding the right dog for search-and-rescue disaster work is no accident. "Many paws are raised, but few are chosen," says Debra Tosch. Labrador and golden retrievers often train well because they're strong, athletic dogs who excel at hunting; but German shepherds, Border collies, and other canines with the right combination of characteristics train well, too.

When selecting potential candidates, trainers look for healthy puppies — ideally between ages two and ten months — who have high energy levels and "live to search."

"These dogs have a strong prey-hunt drive," says Tosch. "Lots of dogs will chase a ball if you throw it, but many will give up if it lands out of sight in some bushes. We want the dog that will leap in the bushes and keep hunting until she finds it."

Other essential traits for search and rescue dogs include:

☆ A friendly disposition toward people and other animals;

☆ A high level of focus on tasks — the dog shouldn't be distracted easily by sounds, etc.;

☆ A willingness to take risks and act against their instincts — for example, remaining on a moving surface instead of jumping off;

☆ A strong play drive — the dog must be motivated to keep working to get a reward, which can be anything from a tug-of-war game to a favorite toy or treat.

"Dogs that we're looking for don't tend to make good pets," says Tosch. "They're constantly putting their nose into everything and bringing you a ball to throw. They really need an outlet for their energy." And search and rescue work is just that outlet!

Left: A chaplain blesses New York Police Department dogs Kiefer and Atlas. The two dogs and their handlers worked many rescue and recovery missions at Ground Zero. Below: President George W. Bush meets with Urban Search and Rescue canines.

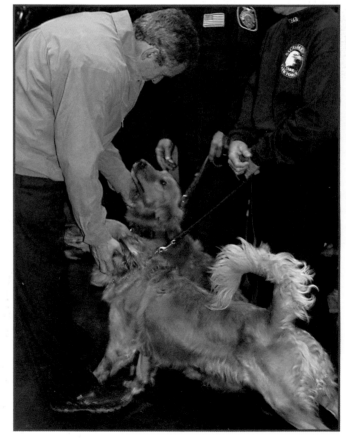

Officer Chris Christensen and his canine partner, Servus, left their Missouri home just hours after terrorists attacked the World Trade Center in New York to join in the search for survivors.

DANGER IN THE RUINS

"Hey dog guy!" someone calls out. "We need a canine . . . there are victims off Liberty Street." Missouri police officer Chris Christensen and his seventy-pound Belgian Malinois, Servus, respond immediately.

"We went to the back side of World Trade Center buildings Four and Five with Rescue Three of the New York Fire Department," says Christensen. Weaving through piles of twisted steel, concrete, and broken glass, Christensen located a small opening leading to an area below Ground Zero. Was someone trapped beneath?

"I went down about eight to ten feet and stood on a little ledge, when something caught my backpack and turned me around," he says. "As this happened, Servus fell past me about twelve to fifteen feet. He literally flew right by me and landed face first into a pile of dust, debris, and broken glass. Of course, his first instinct was to get oxygen, and he inhaled all that dust into his lungs.

"Instantly, you could see the fear in his face. He knew he was in trouble. He started to panic and convulse — he couldn't get the [ashlike] debris out of his nose. By the time I jumped down to get to him, his tongue had turned the brightest purple, and I thought 'my God, this dog is going to die if I don't get him out of here.'"

Christensen immediately went to retrieve Servus. He lifted the dog above his shoulders and placed him on a ledge; then, Christensen climbed up the opening. "My dog's in trouble, I need help!" he screamed.

Fortunately, a fireman nearby responded.

"I passed the dog to him, tossed up my pack, and crawled out," Christensen says. "The first thing I saw was a big fire truck and thought, they must have oxygen, so I ran across the debris field to the truck with the dog in my arms."

Servus's condition deterioriated quickly. "He was fully convulsive, had no eye reflexes, and his chest was rising and falling like a marathon runner's," says Christensen. "We tried to do some suction work but couldn't get all the debris out. When we poured water on his face, something that looked like liquid concrete ran out of his nose. Then one of the nurses asked if I wanted an IV [intravenous fluids], and a fireman hooked it up.

"The next thing I know, we're putting Servus in a basket stretcher and placing him on a damaged car while we run for help. A New York City Police Department van pulls around the corner and sees we're in trouble. 'You need help?' he asks. 'Yes,' I tell him. 'My dog's been hurt, and we need to get him to an animal hospital.'"

While scouring the rubble, Servus fell twelve to fifteen feet into the debris and was injured.

When they arrived at the Animal Medical Center, Servus was rushed to the intensive care unit and into the surgery room, and they gave him drugs to stabilize his breathing. "They cleaned him up and calmed him down." Christensen stayed with Servus in the intensive care unit for several hours and then headed back to Ground Zero with a police officer.

After working at the site awhile, Christensen picked up Servus at the Medical Center. "The two of us went back to Ground Zero and crashed [in a squad car] for a few hours near St. Paul's Church.

"Later that afternoon, I decided to help the guys with the bucket brigade* move debris. So I took my backpack out of the squad car, and guess who jumped out of the car? 'You have to get back in the car, buddy,' I told Servus several times. But he just stood there: he didn't wag his tail, he didn't move. 'You've got to be kidding me!' I said. So I hooked up his lead, and he acted like an excited puppy. It was like, 'Let's go to work, Dad!'"

Even after his near-fatal fall, Servus "begged" his handler to return to work!

Christensen and Servus worked at the site for another seven hours, helping search teams where needed. Today, Servus is retired from search and rescue work — his experiences at the World Trade Center site left him with permanent respiratory problems. To protect dogs working in future disaster sites and determine how the air at the sites may affect humans, researchers supported by the American Kennel Club Health Foundation are monitoring the health of Servus and other search and rescue dogs who worked "the pile." Christensen also has formed an organization called the United States Search & Rescue Dog Association.

* The bucket brigade was a group of people who tried to dig quickly through the piles of rubble at Ground Zero by scooping up debris, placing it in a bucket, and passing it down a human chain.

COMFORTING CANINES

"I can't believe she's here," said Nancy Zuckerman as she buried her face in the keeshond's fluffy coat and wet it with tears. Zuckerman, whose husband, Alan Lederman, died on September 11, was one of about sixty people taking a special boat for families of World Trade Center victims who wished to visit the site and grieve for their loved ones.

"What's her name?" she asked the dog's handler.

"Tikva [TEEK-vah]," replied Cindy Ehlers, president and founder of HOPE Crisis Response AAES (animal assisted emotional support) in Eugene, Oregon.

"Tikva! That means 'hope' in Hebrew, and I'm Jewish," Zuckerman said. She clung to Tikva — a trained therapy dog — and told Ehlers that dogs were the love of her husband's life. "He had a blue merle collie that looked like Tikva," Ehlers says, "and

Top and right: Tikva, a therapy dog from Oregon, offered rescue workers and others emotional relief from the death and destruction at the World Trade Center site.

he kept pictures of the dog at home. That's why [Nancy] connected with my dog. She saw Tikva as a gift from her husband and believed that God had brought Tikva out from Oregon as a sign — to give her hope to get her through this time."

Therapy dogs like Tikva lift people's spirits and provide a safe outlet for their emotions. One reason may be because dogs are nonjudgmental, says Lynnette Spanola of the Delta Society, a Seattle-based organization that brings people and animals together to improve human health. Research shows that dogs have many positive effects on people and can enhance our quality of life. They help us cope with stress, lower our blood pressure, build our self-esteem, and make us feel less lonely.

Therapy dogs work with children in hospitals, seniors in nursing homes, prison inmates, hospice patients, and special-needs students. They also work with victims of emotional trauma, such as those working at the World Trade Center site.

Each day, police officers, firefighters, and other rescue workers faced the overwhelming task of searching for survivors, and eventually for human remains. "They were exhausted and feeling helpless, because it's their job to save people and they weren't able to do it," says Ehlers. To cope, many tucked away their feelings until they felt comfortable acknowledging them. That's where the therapy dogs worked their magic: they engaged and relaxed people in a matter of minutes — something one Red Cross counselor said it would generally take her days to do.

"We were stopped all the time," says Ehlers. "It took us eight hours to go around the site twice. Everyone was reaching out to touch the dogs, pet the dogs, and hug the dogs. One firefighter couldn't believe how soft Tikva was." The touch of her warm fur contrasted sharply with the cold steel he had sifted through in the debris pile.

"Wow, she's so soft," a New York City firefighter says as he hugs Tikva, a furry keeshond. New York firefighters lost hundreds of their colleagues in the terrorist attacks.

Tikva brought a smile to many of the rescue workers' faces. Cindy Ehlers explains that a chemical change takes place in the body when people pet dogs. As a result, people relax and tend to talk more about their experiences.

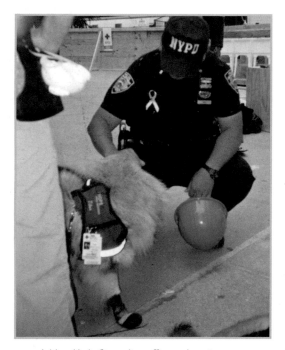

A New York City police officer takes time out to pet Tikva.

CANINE COUNSELORS

"When we first arrived at the site, we were met by police officers and volunteer workers," says Ehlers. "It was much different than going down to Ground Zero. . . . Once we were there, we could see the dogs' moods change. They became more concerned about the people. They were very polite about who they went up to, and wouldn't go unless we said it was okay."

Before the visit, Ehlers had taught Tikva how to approach people. "She'd go over to someone and touch them with her nose. Then she'd sit and wait until I asked her to say 'Hi,' and she'd wave her paw. People thought that was pretty cool. Then if they leaned forward, she'd put her paws up on their lap, and if they leaned forward even more to give her a hug, she'd nuzzle their neck.

"A lot of these people couldn't share what was on their minds with others — they didn't know how to," says Ehlers. "But when they began touching the dogs it relaxed them — some started sharing their experiences right away." Others wanted to help and asked to feed the dogs everything from cookies to hamburgers. "Tikva ate all kinds of foods in New York," Ehlers says.

Tikva is Ehlers's second therapy dog. Her first dog, a keeshond named Bear, worked with her in schools and nursing homes. In May of 1998, the pair began making regular visits to Thurston High School in Springfield, Oregon, following a deadly shooting that left everyone emotionally stunned. "Traumatized people release a scent that dogs immediately pick up," Ehlers says. Bear always knew which students needed her most.

What does it take to be a therapy dog?

Good therapy dogs are generally people-oriented, enjoy being in a variety of situations and environments, and aren't easily ruffled when they hear loud noises or feel someone yanking their tail. According to Assistance Dogs

International Inc., an organization that sets standards for therapy dogs, the dogs must be able to perform basic obedience skills (sit, stay, come, down, and heel) with voice commands and hand signals, and they should not show any signs of aggression. No biting, snapping, growling, jumping on strangers, or begging and sniffing of people.

Handlers also require special skills. They need to work well with their dogs, learn about the needs of the people they're visiting, and know what signs to look for when their canine partners become tired.

Ehlers enjoys working with keeshonds, even though many types of dogs — from purebreds to mixed breeds — may qualify to be therapy dogs. "I really like keeshonds because they have a natural love for kids and people in general," she says. "They were reared on the barges in Holland and their job was to be with the family." She also likes them because they always look like they're smiling and they "have markings on their eyes that look like spectacles. It's a good conversation starter."

Tikva's unique appearance quickly drew the attention of rescue workers at the World Trade Center.

"That's the funniest-looking search and rescue dog I've ever seen," one worker said. "What can she do?" When Ehlers explained that Tikva was a therapy dog, "the workers seemed grateful."

Even more important, after each visit to the site, people would ask again and again: "Will you be back tomorrow?"

Josiah Whitaker and his German shepherd mix, Hoss, joined Cindy Ehlers and Tikva at Ground Zero. Both are part of the HOPE Crisis Response AAES team in Eugene, Oregon.

Chief Roy Gross donated the use of an SPCA mobile hospital van to treat injured animals at Ground Zero.

ANIMAL MASH

Kiefer emerges from Ground Zero dusty, dirty, and a bit dehydrated. The German shepherd has just finished combing through the rubble with his partner, NYPD Officer Chris Hanley. The two head toward a makeshift animal medical station a few blocks away.

"Good boy!" says a veterinarian, patting Kiefer on the back. Several veterinary technicians gather around the dog and Officer Hanley. "What's his name?" "How long has he been working?"

During the first weeks after the World Trade Center attack, dozens of dogs each day passed through the Suffolk County Society for the Prevention of Cruelty to Animals (SPCA) medical station, which was set

Hours after terrorists attacked the World Trade Center on September 11, the Suffolk County SPCA set up a medical station to treat search and rescue dogs.

up the night of September 11 to treat search and rescue canines. Located three blocks from Ground Zero, the station included a mobile animal surgical hospital (MASH) unit — one of only three of its kind in the United States — equipped with several operating tables, X-ray equipment, and a laboratory for analyzing blood and other samples. Outside the hospital van stood several tents lined with tables, each overflowing with donated medical supplies, dog food, booties, chew toys, and treats.

The MASH unit includes a lab and is one of only three of its kind in the United States.

25

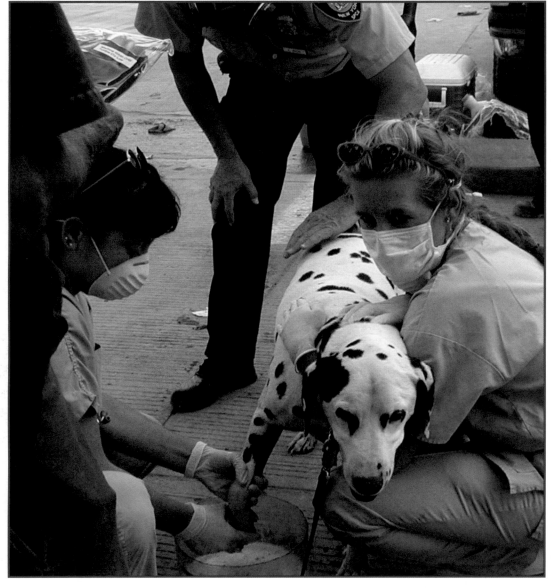

Veterinary volunteers clean the contaminants off a rescue dog's paws.

"When the dogs first came in, they were covered in debris and contaminants, so we washed them down and cleaned the grime off their feet," explains veterinarian John Charos. Their eyes — red and irritated from the dust — were flushed clean and treated with antibiotics. "Then we gave the dogs physical exams and evaluated their overall condition."

Many of the dogs had elevated heart rates. The most common injuries included bloodied paws from metal and glass cuts, burns from the smouldering rubble, breathing difficulties from the dust-laden air, and dehydration from the sweltering heat.

"Most dogs worked twelve-hour shifts," says Charos. "They went into Ground Zero for three hours, came out for an hour or two, then headed back in." To prevent dehydration from the heat, the medical team administered fluids intravenously. "We had IV bags hanging in a row, and treated as many as fifteen dogs at a time," says Chief Roy Gross of the Suffolk County SPCA, who oversaw the MASH unit and coordinated SPCA volunteers.

During the first few days, many dogs became sick with diarrhea and had to eat special dog food. Others refused to eat or drink. Some people say the dogs were frustrated because they failed to find survivors. Others say the dogs mirrored the moods of their handlers, and that the sad feelings "traveled down the leash."

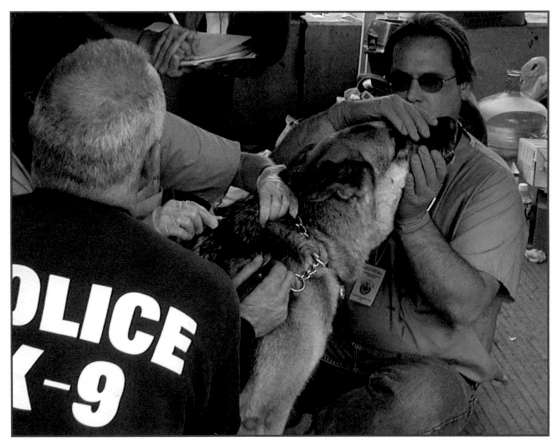

Dr. John Charos checks a police canine's condition after the dog worked "the pile."

Volunteers set up showers and washed dust, dirt, and grime off the rescue dogs working at the World Trade Center site.

A search and rescue dog receives intravenous fluids to prevent dehydration and combat exhaustion.

To lift the dogs' spirits, handlers staged mock rescues and hid in safe spots within the rubble so their dogs could find them and feel successful about their jobs. Squeaky toys and lots of love and praise also kept their tails wagging.

Some of the rescue dogs wore booties to protect their paws from sharp metals and glass in the rubble.

Mary Flood of the Utah Task Force One FEMA Urban Search and Rescue Team took her partner, Jake, for walks and played tug-of-war with him between shifts. Jake, a muscular seventy-eight-pound black Lab who has a slight disability (one of his legs is shorter than the others), also received some relaxing rubdowns from a massage therapist.

"They offered round-the-clock massages for the rescue workers and dogs," Flood says. "The dogs were stiff and tight, too," especially after long days of climbing piles of concrete and crawling into crevices.

Utah search dog Jake enjoys a massage while his handler, Mary Flood, looks on.

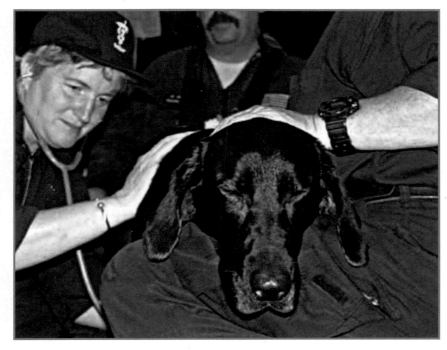

A few days after the terrorist attack in New York, FEMA set up another medical station to treat search and rescue dogs. Here, Dr. H. Marie Suthers McCable works on search dog Kinsay's injured paw. Wounded paws were among the most common canine injuries at Ground Zero.

Partners David Lim and Sirius traveled everywhere together.

TRIBUTE TO A FALLEN HERO

Officer David Lim's work day began like any other. He and his partner, a yellow Labrador retriever named Sirius, badge Number 17, worked out of a basement office in Two World Trade Center, also known as Tower Two. As part of the K-9 police unit for the New York Port Authority, Lim and Sirius — a bomb-sniffing dog — searched for explosives on the site. It was their job to check unattended packages and search cars and trucks as they entered the sprawling seven-building complex. "We were together most all the time," Lim says. "He never complained. Sometimes we'd work long hours, searching hundreds of vehicles, and he'd look at me like, 'What do you want me to do next?'"

Lim and Sirius also secured the area for the arrival of important people, including the former president of the United States. In September of 2000 the two met Bill Clinton, who asked to pet Sirius. Another time, they met Minnesota Governor Jesse Ventura. Their most important achievement, however, was that no explosives had ever detonated under their watch.

That is, until September 11, 2001. At 8:46 A.M. Lim received reports of an explosion on the upper floors of One World Trade Center.

"They must have gotten one by us," a concerned Lim said to Sirius, thinking that a bomb had gone off. Lim didn't know it yet, but terrorists had hijacked American Airlines Flight 11 from Boston and crashed the plane into Tower One.

He put Sirius into the kennel and raced upstairs to investigate the situation.

"You stay there," he had told his K-9 partner before leaving. "I'll be right back for you."

Sirius meets President Clinton on September 11, 2000, exactly one year before terrorists attacked the World Trade Center.

TERROR IN TOWER ONE

Officer Lim ran to Tower One, the top now engulfed in smoke and flames, and headed up the narrow stairwell as frightened evacuees clambered to get down. "They needed the most help on the upper floors," he says. When Lim reached the 27th floor, he called his wife, Diane, and she told him that a plane had hit the building. "I'm going up," he told her. "Be careful," she replied.

At the sky lobby on the 44th floor, Lim warned people in line not to take the elevators because the power could go out. "All of a sudden, a second plane hits Tower Two, and I see this fireball descending from the upper floors of the other building, right in front of my window," he says. "The fireball moves down, blows out the windows and knocks us on our butts."

The lights flicker and people panic. Officer Lim and the others quickly head down the stairs, with Lim checking each floor for remaining workers as he descends. "Somewhere between the twentieth and fortieth floors, Tower Two collapses and our building starts shaking," he says. "I figured if that one-hundred-ten-story building can come down, so can ours."

When he reached the fifth floor, Officer Lim met firefighters from Ladder Company 6 in Chinatown and a woman named Josephine Harris, whom they were helping down the stairs. The woman had walked down from the 73rd floor and was struggling with each step. In the stairwell on the fourth floor, an exhausted Josephine said she couldn't go on anymore.

Just then, the building rumbled. *This is it,* Lim thought, *Tower One's collapsing.* "It felt like an avalanche as the floors compressed and pushed the air down." Steel, glass, drywall, and concrete swirled everywhere, and Lim was "just waiting for a huge chunk of debris" to hit him. "It felt like an eternity, but it must have lasted about fifteen seconds," he says.

Then the debris stopped falling, and a thick cloud of gray dust settled on Lim and the others. Miraculously, they had lived through the crumbling of Tower One with only minor injuries.

A PROMISE KEPT

Hours later, firefighters from Ladder Company 43 rescued the group from the rubble. "The medics checked me out," Lim says, "then I told them that I had to get back to Tower Two so I could rescue my dog. 'He's my partner,' I said."

Lim tried several times to get to Sirius in the basement office, but rescue workers wouldn't allow him to re-enter the building. "Building Seven, nearby, was still on fire and they didn't want to take any chances," he says.

In the days that followed, doctors kept Officer Lim from searching "the pile" at the World Trade Center site. They worried about the emotional toll it could have on him. "My only hope was that Sirius had died quickly," Lim says. "I didn't want him to suffer." In the meantime, Lim kept tabs on the rescue effort, regularly checking to see if workers had reached the kennel. During that time, he received hundreds of emails and cards from people offering their condolences, and more than 150 offers of a new dog.

More than 100 police handlers and their dogs paid tribute to Sirius at a memorial in Liberty State Park on April 24, 2002.

On January 21, 2002, rescue workers found Sirius's remains and immediately contacted Lim. All the evidence indicated that he died instantly when the kennel collapsed. As befits a hero, Sirius's body was removed with full police honors and a prayer.

"I carried him out with another officer, and everyone lined up and saluted Sirius as we left," Lim says. "All the great machines were silent as we led the procession to the police truck, and I was given the American flag that draped his body. I will cherish it always. It was a tough day, but at least I fulfilled the promise I made to him on September 11. Sirius waited, and I came back."

Across the Hudson River from the World Trade Center site, bagpipes and a 21-gun salute honored the only on-duty police canine known to have died during the September 11 terrorist attacks.

Sirius was named after the brightest star in the constellation of Canis Major (the Big Dog), which is nicknamed the Dog Star.

MORE AMAZING CANINES

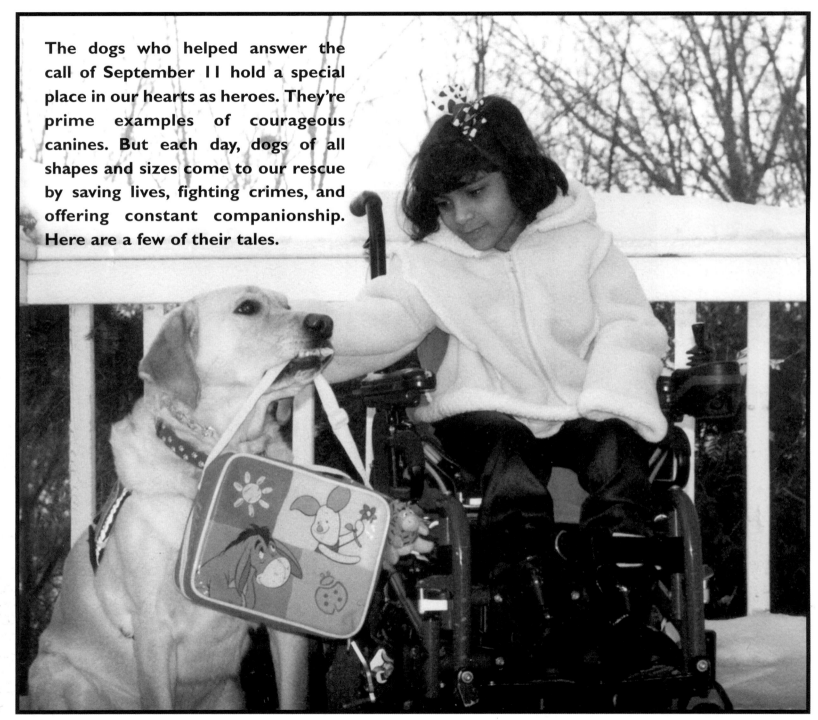

The dogs who helped answer the call of September 11 hold a special place in our hearts as heroes. They're prime examples of courageous canines. But each day, dogs of all shapes and sizes come to our rescue by saving lives, fighting crimes, and offering constant companionship. Here are a few of their tales.

Sunni Forty and her skilled companion dog, Roan, are the best of friends. "Roan helps Sunni dress and undress," says her mom, Wendy. "He carries Sunni's lunch box at school, and he opens doors and retrieves things Sunni drops." He's also a great companion and "is even better than a stuffed animal to sleep with."

A member of the Beagle Brigade sniffs an international traveler's bag for prohibited fruit and meat.

THE BEAGLE BRIGADE

Mugsy knew something was up. He could smell it in the air, or at least in the small suitcase the woman carried into the Atlanta airport. So he sat by the bag to alert his handler, Lisa Beckett.

"Are you carrying any fruits, vegetables, or meat?" Beckett asked the woman. "No," she replied.

Beckett checked the woman's Customs Declaration Card to see if she had declared any items. No food or other agricultural products had been declared.

Hmmm, Beckett thought. *Mugsy's not letting go of this one.*

Turns out, Mugsy's nose knew best. After a thorough search of the woman's luggage, inspectors found that she had tried to smuggle sausage in from another country by sewing it into the lining of her suitcase! If that sausage had contained the virus for foot-and-mouth disease, which debilitates cattle, it could have cost the country billions of dollars.

Fortunately, Mugsy and more than sixty Beagle Brigade teams are on the job at twenty-one international airports across the United States. These furry inspectors for the U.S. Department of Agriculture (USDA) sniff luggage and packages after each flight, looking for food contraband.

"Most of the people who bring in food items aren't aware

Lisa Beckett and her dog, Mugsy, helped seize food contraband in Atlanta. Now Beckett trains other beagles and their handlers to do the same at the USDA National Detector Dog Training Center in Orlando, Florida.

Beagles sit to alert their handlers when they smell agricultural products. When they make a find, the dogs receive a food treat.

that it's illegal," Beckett says. "It never occurs to them that they may contain harmful insects or diseases, so the beagles help increase awareness." But every now and then someone will try to sneak in a delicacy, and that can be a real problem. It's thought that just one orange carried by a traveler may have introduced the Mediterranean fruit fly to California in 1980 — a pest that took more than $100 milllion to wipe out.

WHY BEAGLES?

When you think of detector dogs, beagles generally don't come to mind first. But it turns out they're the perfect airport detectives. "Beagles are naturally friendly," Beckett says, "and their noses are equal to or better than other breeds'." They're also small, so they don't intimidate travelers.

Most important, beagles love food. They really love food. That's why, unlike many other working dogs, they're rewarded with treats. "We train them for five weeks on scent discrimination," explains Beckett. "Odors we begin with include apples, oranges, mango, beef, and pork."

Training for the Beagle Brigade begins with basic scents such as citrus and beef hidden in boxes. During their careers, some dogs learn to sniff out about 50 different odors.

To help the beagles distinguish between foods, trainers place various scents in boxes. "Some boxes have odors we want them to respond to; some boxes have odors that we don't want them to respond to," Beckett says. "When they sniff a box that has an odor we want them to respond to, we praise them and give them a treat. And when they sniff a box that has, say, chocolate cake in it, we ignore it. Pretty soon, they realize that 'when I sniff this one, I get a treat.'"

After six months to a year, the beagles boast an eighty percent accuracy rate; and after two years of experience, they're accurate ninety percent of the time. The Beagle Brigade has seized an average of 75,000 prohibited food products a year. "The program's so successful we're doubling the teams we have in the United States, and we're helping other countries begin their own programs," Beckett says.

Left: Stefanie, Alette, and Carol-Ann De Maio Goheen form a skilled companion team, with Mom as the "alpha," or leader of the pack. While Alette is a companion to Stefanie, she follows the commands of Carol-Ann. Right: Alette is a bridge to friendship for Stefanie, who was born with cerebral palsy.

ALETTE: COMPANION FOR LIFE

Stefanie Goheen's face brightens with a smile as her companion dog, Alette (rhymes with "spaghetti"), settles down beside her hot-pink wheelchair. The pretty thirteen-year-old lifts the dog's leash and extends it to a woman nearby. "Come share my dog," she signals with her actions, because words are not her mode of communication. Born with cerebral palsy — a disorder caused by a brain injury that affects a person's muscle control — Stefanie cannot speak. Yet, with the help of an assistance dog trained by an organization called Canine Companions for Independence (CCI), she can quickly connect to others in friendship.

"Alette's a bridge," explains Stefanie's mom, Carol-Ann De Maio Goheen. "Stefanie's not your typical kid, and even good-hearted people aren't sure what to do around her. But everyone knows what to do with a dog. People will come

Alette lived with a puppy raiser for the first year of her life, learning basic obedience and social skills so she could one day become an assistance dog.

Puppy raiser Carol Ann Arnim and her former roommate, Alette, reunite on graduation day. While the two said their good-byes again a few hours later, they still visit each other several times a year.

up to us in grocery stores and malls. And, at school, Alette helps Stefanie engage with other children." An illness that once isolated the teenager from her peers now accentuates her specialness in a positive way.

Since joining the Goheen family on Saint Patrick's Day of 2001, Alette, a three-year-old golden retriever and Labrador retriever mix, has been a constant companion to Stefanie. The two even cuddle together at night — both with their heads on a pillow.

"Before Alette arrived, Stefanie woke up seven or eight times a night and needed to be calmed back to sleep," says her mother. "Now Stefanie sleeps through most nights. She probably still wakes up, but then snuggles up to the dog to relax."

One time, Alette awakened Ms. Goheen in the middle of the night. "She was agitated and stressed, so she came to me as the leader of the pack [or alpha dog]." To her surprise, Ms. Goheen found Stefanie in the middle of a small seizure, coughing and gasping for air. "Alette must have noticed Stefanie's irregular breathing and wanted to protect her."

BORN TO SERVE

Like most dogs at CCI, Alette was bred especially for work as an assistance dog and spent the first eight weeks of her life with a breeder-caretaker in California. Soon after, she moved to Arizona to live with her puppy raiser, volunteer Carol Ann Arnim.

"Alette's an incredible dog," says Arnim, who was grieving the death of her husband when she took in the puppy. "She has a healing energy about her that helped heal my heart. Now she's doing the same for Stefanie and her mother."

After learning basic obedience commands with Arnim and being exposed to a variety of social environments, Alette returned to CCI for ten months of advanced training — a move that's stressful for both the dog and the puppy raiser. "Only about thirty to forty percent of the dogs make it through advanced training to graduation," says Arnim. "But I knew from the beginning that Alette would graduate."

Some dogs are released because they fail their health exams — assistance dogs must be strong and capable of working about eight years. Others show excessive stress or fear and aren't able to calm down and recover quickly. "None of the released dogs is considered a failure," says Arnim. They experience a "career change," with the puppy raiser given the first option to adopt them into a new life.

During advanced training, Alette learned how to work around a wheelchair, retrieve items, and press buttons for elevators and wheelchair access doors. More specifically, she learned how to work as a skilled companion — a dog who could take commands from one person (Ms. Goheen) and be an affectionate friend to another (Stefanie).

Stefanie and Alette play ball — after all, Alette is a retriever!

Skilled companion dogs are one of four types of assistance canines that CCI trains. The others are:

⭐ **Service dogs,** who help people with physical disabilities perform tasks such as retrieving dropped items, pulling a wheelchair, and turning light switches on and off;

⭐ **Facility dogs,** who work with professionals in group settings to help improve the lives of people who have mental, physical, and emotional problems;

⭐ **Hearing dogs,** who alert the deaf and hard-of-hearing to everyday sounds such as doorbells, alarm clocks, and smoke alarms.

Once Alette passed the advanced training, CCI paired her with Stefanie and her mom during a two-week team training session. Here, the Goheens learned how to care for and handle Alette. Among the commands they practiced during team training were:

⭐ **Here:** tells the dog to come and sit in front of you and remain there until the next command is given;

⭐ **Don't:** tells the dog to stop doing something;

⭐ **Hurry:** tells the dog to "go to the bathroom";

Alette helps Stefanie feel less isolated in her illness by offering unconditional love.

⭐ **Dress:** tells the dog to calmly place its head through the training cape collar;

⭐ **Car:** tells the dog to get into a vehicle;

⭐ **Back:** tells the dog to walk backward;

⭐ **Hold:** tells the dog to hold an object until told to release it.

Ms. Goheen also learned how to manage Alette in public. According to CCI, the dog should always be dressed in her vest, attached to a leash and on her best behavior. Alette should never sniff people or initiate contact without permission.

Likewise, Ms. Goheen learned her rights and what to expect from others regarding assistance-dog etiquette. "The Americans with Disabilities Act guarantees people with disabilities the right to be accompanied by a service animal in all areas open to the general public," says CCI spokesperson Peter Rapalus. When meeting a skilled companion team, people should ask for permission before petting the dog, and they should never offer food, whistle loudly, or try to distract the dog from its job.

On graduation day, puppy trainer Carol Ann Arnim tearfully turned over Alette's leash. But she and CCI remain an important part of the Goheen family's life. Follow-up training, class reunions, and frequent phone calls keep everybody connected. As does the golden-haired animal that brought them all together — a dog named Alette.

Jake sniffs for explosives in a women's locker room. His human partner, Gerry Fornino, is an FBI special agent bomb technician.

JAKE: FBI EXPLOSIVES SPECIALIST

Bombs. Fireworks. Guns.

Jake has sniffed them all out in his career as a chemical explosives dog. His handler, Gerry Fornino, is an FBI special agent bomb technician, and together he and Jake search for explosives before they detonate and injure people.

Jake has sniffed for bombs under stadium seats at Superbowl XXXII in San Diego, ensuring the safety of thousands of fans. He's checked out suspicious packages anonymously left in ambulance vans after the World Trade Center attacks. He's investigated the wreckage of airplane crashes, including TWA Flight 800, which exploded in mid-air over Long Island Sound in 1996, and EgyptAir 990, which plunged into the Atlantic Ocean over Nantucket Island, Massachusetts, in 1999. In both cases, Jake sniffed for signs of foul play — any residue of explosives that might indicate a bomb had brought down the planes. Neither investigation proved conclusive.

An eight-year-old Labrador retriever, Jake began training to be an FBI canine agent at about six months. Labs are especially suited to bomb sniffing, Fornino says, because they tend to have a lot of energy, which they use to search relentlessly for objects. Today, Jake can sniff out anywhere from 12 to 20 major explosive chemicals and can recognize up to 19,000 different combinations

Gerry and Jake have worked on assignments involving everything from the Miss America Pageant in Branson, Missouri, to the World Economic Summit in Denver.

Like this bomb-sniffing dog in training, Jake spent his early years learning to recognize the scents of different explosives.

of these in even the slightest amounts. "Many explosives contain nitroglycerin, so Jake often picks up on that," Fornino says.

Most FBI explosives-detection dogs spend at least ten weeks learning to identify explosive chemicals. Instructors at the Bureau of Alcohol, Tobacco and Firearms (ATF) use a "training wheel" to teach dogs. The tool consists of four containers on a rotating wheel. One container holds an explosive, while the others are empty or planted with an unrelated odor to distract the dog. Upon finding the explosive chemical, the dog is rewarded, and the process begins again.

Unlike search and rescue dogs, who bark to signal a find, explosives-detection dogs signal with a "passive" response. In Jake's case, he stops and sits near the site with the strongest scent. "It wouldn't be a good idea to have him jump up and down near an explosive," Fornino says. "He absolutely needs to be under control and not come in direct contact with any device."

When Jake makes a find, he gets to play ball as a reward. "He'll do just about anything to play ball," Fornino says. Some of the more unusual places people have hidden bombs include children's toys, bicycles, and yard decorations.

Sometimes just the sight of Jake scares people. "When I'm in an airport traveling with Jake, I notice that some people waiting in line — even long ones — head straight for the bathroom. I suspect that a few of them are flushing drugs down the toilet, thinking that Jake's a drug-sniffing dog. But if it keeps them from bringing the stuff on the airplane, that's fine by me."

Jake loves his work. "He's very methodical and focused when he's on the job," says his proud partner. "No machine can compete with his nose." That's important because people's lives depend on his special skills. "Bomb-sniffing dogs receive the highest level of training," Fornino says. And, ultimately, they may have to make the highest sacrifice.

"When you're searching a truck with 5,000 pounds of explosives in the back of it, you're reminded that your dog may one day give up his life to save people that you don't even know," says Fornino. It's difficult to think about, but it's all in a day's work for an FBI canine special agent.

Gerry and Jake worked security for Superbowl XXXII at Qualcomm Stadium in San Diego.

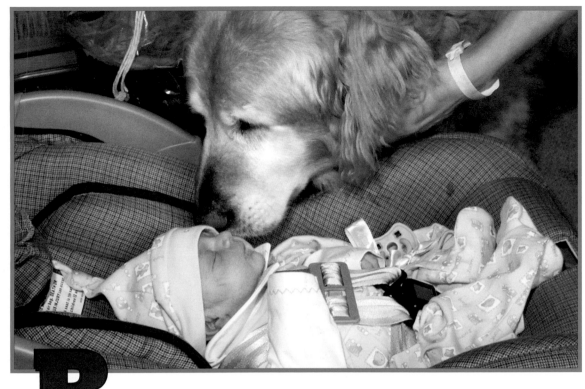

Bullet welcomes Troy Joseph home from the hospital.

BULLET: A BABY BOY'S BEST FRIEND

Not all hero dogs receive special training for their work. Some, such as Bullet, are family pets who instinctively rise to the occasion in an emergency. . . .

Bullet raced to the kitchen, barking excitedly. "What's wrong?" asked Pam Sica, who was warming a bottle for her three-week-old son, Troy Joseph. "Do you need to go out?" The golden retriever continued barking and darted anxiously between the kitchen and a hallway that led to the baby's bedroom. "He kept looking at me, turning around and going into the hallway," says Mrs. Sica. "So I ran after him into the bedroom."

Bullet saved Troy Joseph's life when he noticed a change in the baby's breathing pattern and alerted mom Pam Sica.

People showered Bullet with dog gifts and treats after hearing about his heroism. Below: Three years before Bullet saved Troy Joseph's life, the Sica family saved his by paying $5,000 for an operation to remove a softball-sized tumor from his liver.

There, the new mother discovered her son with his head thrown back, gurgling and gasping for air. "I picked him up and saw that he was turning shades of red to blue to purple," says Mrs. Sica. "Then his little body collapsed in my arms."

Mrs. Sica screamed for her husband, who was showering. Troy Lawrence — who thought his son was choking — immediately turned the baby upside down and patted him on the back. When that didn't work, he administered CPR while Mrs. Sica called 911. Within minutes paramedics arrived, gave the baby oxygen, and stabilized his condition before rushing him in an ambulance to a nearby hospital.

Doctors later diagnosed Troy Joseph with double pneumonia (pneumonia in both lungs), and discovered that he had two holes in his heart — one that is common in babies and would eventually close on its own, and another that would probably require an operation.

"Bullet saved Troy Joseph's life," says Mrs. Sica. "The paramedics told my husband that if we had found him seconds later, we may have lost him."

Mr. and Mrs. Sica are not sure how Bullet knew that Troy Joseph was in trouble, but they believe the dog's keen senses probably detected changes in the baby's normal behavior and prompted him to alert them. Perhaps the fifteen-year-old canine wanted to return a favor.

Three years earlier, the Sica family had rescued him from near death. During the dog's annual exam, the vet had found a pea-sized tumor on Bullet's liver, which quickly grew to the size of a softball. "I asked the doctor what would happen if we didn't operate, and he said Bullet would bleed to death," says Mrs. Sica. "I couldn't let that happen." So, despite doubts from friends and family — "they thought we were 'crazy' to spend five thousand dollars on a dog that might not live through the operation" — the Sicas borrowed the money for the surgery and Bullet fully recovered.

"It's pretty amazing," says Mrs. Sica. "If we didn't save his life, he wouldn't have been around to save my Troy Joseph's."

Doc: Lifesaver on the Slopes

Doc, an avalanche rescue dog, helped save the life of skier Jeff Eckland, who was trapped in the trees after triggering a snow slide at Kirkwood Ski Resort in California.

Jeff Eckland hiked above the lifts at Kirkwood Ski Resort in California. It was a Monday morning in January, and he and a few friends wanted to get in some good runs after having worked the snow-grooming machines that weekend.

"I was on skis, and my friends were snowboarding," says Eckland. "It took them a lot longer to get ready, so I decided to go down first." Seconds after he did, a slab of snow broke loose. At first, Eckland thought he had set off a small slide — no problem, he'd skied through these before. Then his skis popped off. "At that point, I was crawling on top of the snow, sort of like dog-paddling in water, and waiting for it to stop," he says.

Instead, the slide picked up speed. Eckland heard a loud roar and "the whole mountain gave way. It was super-fast acceleration," he says. "All I remember is glancing up and seeing a bank of trees about a hundred yards away. The next time I looked up they were right in my face."

Trapped near the trees, Eckland felt the avalanche rumble past him. "It was a weird sensation. I could feel the snow pushing me up the tree, and then as it went by, I could feel the snow pushing me down," he says.

Suddenly everything stopped. "It was quiet, and I was in tons of pain," Eckland says. "I thought a juniper branch had gone through my abdomen, because I could smell fresh sap."

Eckland couldn't move a finger. He didn't know up from down. "I was packed in really tight," he says. Still, he had confidence that his friends saw what had happened and were calling for help. "I figured that as long as I tried to relax and conserve my oxygen, I'd be all right."

When Jeff Eckland realized that Doc had saved his life, he paid tribute to the golden retriever by keeping his image close to his heart.

SNOW-SEARCH

Eckland's intuition was on target. His friends had watched the slide and raced for help. "I was about ten minutes away from the site when the call came in," says ski patroller Dave Paradysz. "'Avalanche with a person caught.'"

"Doc knew something was going on right away," Paradysz says. "He was real excited and ready to go. So I splashed some water on him [their regular routine] and he was out like a gun. Immediately, he went ripping into the trees and started digging on this pile of snow in front of them." The golden retriever then spun around and moved into the shadows on the other side of the trees, where Paradysz couldn't see him. "When I got to the other side, Doc was on his hind legs digging frantically. His tail whirled round and round like a propeller."

Meanwhile Eckland, now buried in the snow for almost fifteen minutes, began to panic. "I was hyperventilating and breathing like crazy, but there wasn't much air left. Then I started to get tunnel vision, where I couldn't see anything but the difference between light and dark. It was getting darker, darker, and darker, and right at that moment, Doc's paw hit my back. I knew right away it was a dog's paw. I couldn't hear anything until his paw broke through, then all of a sudden a rush of air broke, and I could hear a dog whimpering excitedly. It felt so good to have those claws digging into my back."

Paradysz moved Doc aside to see what he was digging at and saw that it was Eckland's back smashed up against the tree. He located the skier's head and pumped oxygen to him down the narrow tunnel Doc had burrowed. As rescuers continued to dig, it became clear: the avalanche had folded Eckland's body backward — heels to ears — and buried him under five feet of snow!

During the three months it took Eckland's back to heal, the story of his rescue unfolded. "I realized that if Doc wasn't there, I would have been dead," Eckland says. "Once I realized that, I had to do something." So he did.

Eckland visited Doc that spring, played some ball, and took some pictures of his canine hero. The next fall, he returned to work at the ski resort with a surprise. Tattooed on his chest was a color portrait of Doc — right above his heart.

RESOURCES

To learn more about Hero Dogs, check out the resources below.

Books

• *War Dogs* by Jeanette Sanderson (Apple, May 1997)

• *Working Dogs: Tales from Animal Planet's K-9 to 5 World* by Colleen Needles and Kit Carlson, photographs by Kim Levin (Discovery Books, 2000)

Web Sites

• **American Kennel Club:** www.akc.org

• **American Society for the Prevention of Cruelty to Animals (ASPCA):** www.aspca.org

• **ATF's Kid's Page on chemical explosives dogs:** www.atf.treas.gov/kids/canines.htm

• **Canine Companions for Independence:** www.caninecompanions.org

• **Delta Society:** www.deltasociety.org

• **FBI Working Dogs:** www.fbi.gov/kids/dogs/doghome.htm

• **FEMA — Canines' Role in Search and Rescue:** www.fema.gov/usr/usr_canines.htm

• **Guide Dogs for the Blind:** www.guidedogs.com

• **HOPE Crisis Response AAES (animal assisted emotional support):** www.hopeaacr.org

• **K-9 History: The Dogs of War!:** community-2.webtv.net/Hahn-50thAP-K9/K9History

• **K-9 Disaster Relief (Frank Shane and Nikie):** www.K-9DisasterRelief.org

• **National Disaster Search Dog Foundation:** www.ndsdf.org

• **Suffolk County SPCA:** www.suffolkspca.org/index.html

• **USDA Beagle Brigade:** www.aphis.usda.gov/oa/pubs/detdogs.html

Museum Exhibit

Dogs: Wolf, Myth, Hero & Friend

Traveling exhibition created by the Natural History Museum of Los Angeles County (www.nhm.org). For information about the national tour, call 213-763-3517.

Sources Page 6: Phillips, Angus, *Our Bond with Dogs: A Love Story. National Geographic* (January 2002): pp. 12–31. Pages 8, 9: Michael Hingson quotes from "The Path to Safety: A Survivor of the World Trade Center Tragedy Tells His Story." *Guide Dog News* (Fall 2001). Page 9: Life Magazine Staff, *One Nation: America Remembers September 11, 2001.* New York: Little, Brown and Company, 2001. Pages 39, 40: Training information provided by Peter Rapalus of Canine Companions for Independence and the CCI Web site: www.caninecompanions.org.

GLOSSARY

Air-scenting canine • a search dog trained to follow any human scent in an area to its source.

American Society for the Prevention of Cruelty to Animals (ASPCA) • an organization that promotes the welfare of animals and works to prevent them from pain and suffering.

Assistance Dogs International, Inc. • an organization that sets the training standards for therapy and assistance dogs.

Avalanche rescue dog • a dog trained to find people buried in snow. When avalanche dogs pinpoint a human scent, they dig until they locate its source.

Beagle Brigade • teams of detector dogs (contraband dogs) and their human partners who work at international airports to prevent prohibited fruits, plants, and meats from entering the country.

Bucket Brigade • a group of people who tried to quickly dig through the piles of rubble at the World Trade Center site by scooping up debris, placing it in a bucket, and passing it down a human chain.

Bureau of Alcohol, Tobacco and Firearms (ATF) • a law enforcement agency within the U.S. Department of the Treasury. Among its responsibilities are to protect the public and reduce violent crime. One way they do this is to train explosives-detection dogs.

Canine • a member of the dog family.

Canine Companions for Independence (CCI) • an organization that enhances the lives of people with disabilities by providing highly trained assistance dogs.

Delta Society • an organization that brings people and animals together to improve human health.

Explosives-detection dog • a highly trained dog who sniffs out a variety of materials used to make bombs and other explosives.

Facility dog • a highly trained dog who works with professionals in group settings to help improve the lives of people who have mental, physical, and emotional problems.

FEMA (Federal Emergency Management Agency) • the government agency created in 1979 to help people before and after a disaster has been declared by the president of the United States. Disasters the agency has responded to include hurricanes, tornadoes, floods, earthquakes, the Oklahoma City bombing, and the terrorist attacks on the World Trade Center and the Pentagon.

Ground Zero • a commonly used term for the World Trade Center site in New York after it was attacked by terrorists. It generally refers to a site that has been bombed.

Guide dog • a highly trained dog that, under the direction of its visually impaired handler, helps him or her get from one place to another safely.

Guide Dogs for the Blind • an organization that provides guide dogs to the visually impaired in the United States and Canada.

Handler • a working dog's human partner.

Hearing dog • a highly trained dog who alerts the deaf and hard-of-hearing to everyday sounds such as doorbells, alarm clocks, and smoke alarms.

Intraveneous (IV) fluids • fluids given to humans or animals through their veins to keep them hydrated.

Kennel • a house for a dog.

National Disaster Search Dog Foundation (NDSDF) • a California-based organization that finds, trains, and matches disaster search dogs to handlers.

Pads • thick, rough skin on the soles of a dog's paws that provide traction and shock absorbtion.

Pentagon • headquarters for the U.S. Department of Defense, located outside of Washington, D.C. It houses 23,000 employees.

Port Authority of New York and New Jersey • agency that serves the transportation needs of the New York–New Jersey metropolitan region.

Puppy raiser • volunteer who provides basic obedience training and socialization for potential assistance dogs during their first year.

Red Cross • an international organization that assists victims of disasters by helping to ease their suffering. The American Red Cross works closely with FEMA when a major crisis occurs.

FEMA-Certified Urban Search and Rescue (USAR) dog • a highly trained dog who helps to locate survivors in diasaters such as earthquakes and terrorist attacks.

Service dog • a highly trained dog who works with people who have physical disabilities. These canines perform practical tasks, including opening doors, turning on light switches, and retrieving items such as the phone.

Suffolk County SPCA (Society for the Prevention of Cruelty to Animals) • the New York agency that set up a Mobile Animal Surgical Hospital, or MASH unit, and medically cared for the search and rescue dogs working at Ground Zero.

"The pile" • a commonly used term for the mountain of debris left at World Trade Center site in New York after it was attacked by terrorists.

Therapy dog • a dog trained to help comfort people and lift their spirits.

Tracking dog • a dog trained to follow a specific person's unique scent.

USDA • United States Department of Agriculture.

Veterinarian • an animal doctor.

War dog • a highly trained dog who works for the military and does everything from detecting mines to guarding troops.

World Trade Center • a complex of seven buildings on sixteen acres in downtown Manhattan, constructed and operated by the Port Authority of New York and New Jersey. The twin towers, One and Two World Trade Center, both stood 110 stories high and were located at the center of the complex.